MONSTER MATHS

SUBTRACTION

WRITTEN BY
MADELINE TYLER

ILLUSTRATED BY
AMY LI

BookLife PUBLISHING

©2022
BookLife Publishing Ltd.
King's Lynn
Norfolk, PE30 4LS, UK

ISBN: 978-1-83927-252-3

Written by:
Madeline Tyler

Edited by:
John Wood

Designed/Illustrated by:
Amy Li

All rights reserved.
Printed in Poland.

A catalogue record for this book is available from the British Library. All facts, statistics, web addresses and URLs in this book were verified as valid and accurate at time of writing. No responsibility for any changes to external websites or references can be accepted by either the author or publisher.

PHOTO CREDITS

All images courtesy of Shutterstock.com. With thanks to Getty Images, Thinkstock Photo and iStockphoto.

Cover, Page 1 & Page 2 – memphisslim, jojje, Dmitrijj Skorobogatov, Abscent, ag1100. Recurring images throughout – jojje (grid), Dmitrijj Skorobogatov (illustration texture), Abscent (pattern), ag1100 (paper texture), wk1003mike (wood texture) Corey Frey (Monster texture), arigato (carpet texture), cluckva (wallpaper texture), Amy Li (all illustrations). Dog textures – Cinemarama (pink), Krakenimages.com (orange), Lertsakwiman (yellow), Koli-dzei (green), Svetlana.ls (red), Corey Frey (browns). Red room (p3, 8, 12, 16) – Curly Pat, sum-roeng, chinnapan, Africa Studio, Darren Pullman. Park (p4, 22) – Claudio Divizia, SusaZoom. Bokeh Blur Background, Alexander Mazurkevich, Kriengsuk Prasroetsung. Lounge (p6–7, 20) – kidstudio852, arigato, Constantin Seltea, p20–21 – solarus, Kues.

Meeny wants a monster dog.

Meeny wants to keep them all.

This monster can take 1 dog.

7 subtract 1 is 6.

Now there are 6 dogs left.

1
2
3
4
5
6

These monsters can take 2.

6 take away 2 makes 4.

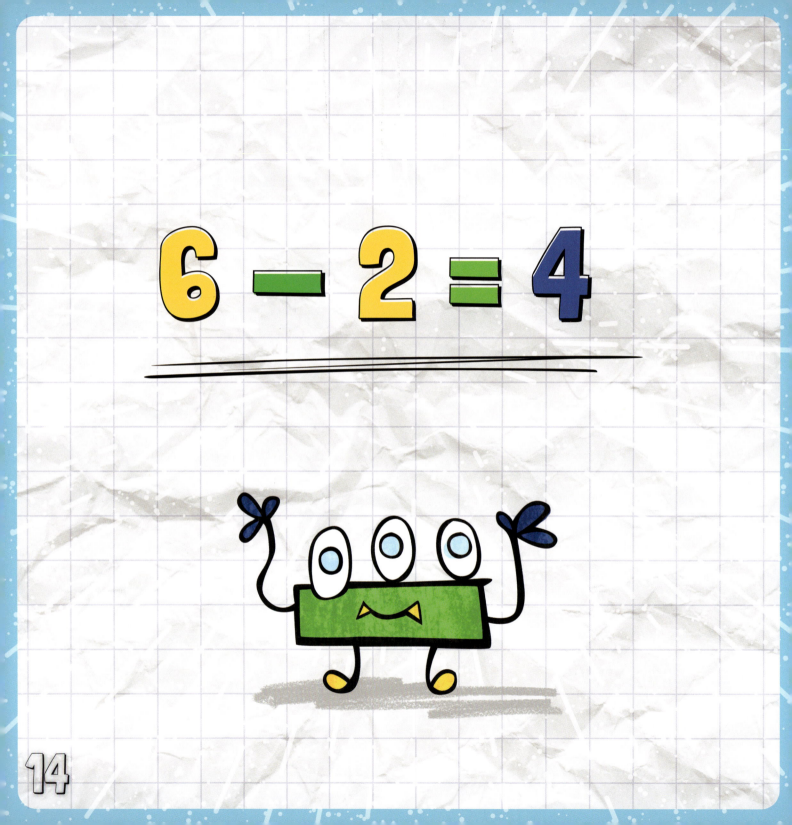

Now there are 4 dogs left.

This monster can take 3.

Now there is 1 dog left.

1 is not too many!

Meeny has 1 monster dog.